new penthouse design

daab

Vivir en un ático supone disfrutar de un lugar privilegiado. La popularización del ascensor, creado a mediados del siglo XIX, trajo consigo un cambio de prioridades en la elección de una vivienda. Al desaparecer el esfuerzo físico necesario para llegar al último piso, los áticos cambiaron su estatus y se convirtieron en las viviendas más deseadas. Desde un ático cambia el punto de vista que se tiene de la ciudad; es posible contemplarla desde las alturas, sentirla y vivirla de forma diferente a cuando se camina por sus calles. Estas construcciones permiten disfrutar de mucha más luz y también de grandes vistas. Además, en muchas ocasiones los áticos cuentan con terrazas u otros espacios exteriores que añaden valor a la vivienda. Esta selección muestra áticos actuales e innovadores, que armonizan con la personalidad de sus habitantes y que han sido diseñados para sacar el máximo provecho de sus especiales características.

Vivre sous les toits suppose de jouir d'un lieu privilégié. La popularisation de l'ascenseur, apparu au milieu du XIXème siècle, a entraîné une évolution des priorités dans le choix d'une demeure. Disparu l'effort physique nécessaire pour atteindre le dernier étage, les mansardes changèrent de statut pour se convertir en logements les plus convoités. Sous les toits, le point de vue sur la ville se transforme : il devient possible de la contempler depuis les hauteurs, de la ressentir et de la vivre d'une manière différente à celle de nos déambulations dans ses rues. Ces constructions permettent de profiter de beaucoup de lumière et de superbes panoramas. En outre, très souvent, les appartements sous les toits comportent des terrasses ou autres espaces extérieurs source de valeur ajoutée. Cette sélection expose quelques logements actuels et novateurs, s'harmonisant avec la personnalité de leurs habitants et pensés pour tirer le parti maximum de leurs caractéristiques spéciales.

Vivere in un attico significa godere di un luogo privilegiato. La popolarizzazione dell'ascensore, creato verso la metà del XIX sec. portò con sé un cambio di priorità nella scelta di un'abitazione. Scomparendo lo sforzo fisico necessario per arrivare all'ultimo piano, gli attici cambiarono il loro status trasformandosi nelle abitazioni più desiderate. Visto da un attico il punto di vista che si ha di una città cambia; è possibile ammirarla dall'alto, sentirla e viverla in maniera diversa da quando si cammina per le sue strade. Queste costruzioni permettono di godere di molta luce ed anche di grandi vedute. In molte occasioni, inoltre, gli attici dispongono di terrazze o di altri spazi esterni che aggiungono valore all'immobile. La presente selezione mostra attici attuali e innovativi, in armonia con la personalità dei loro abitanti e che sono stati disegnati per sfruttare al massimo le loro speciali caratteristiche.

Ein Penthouse ist ein besonders schöner Ort zum Wohnen. Die Erfindung des Fahrstuhls Mitte des 19. Jh. wirkte sich stark auf die Wahl der Wohnung aus. Da keine physischen Anstrengungen mehr notwendig waren, um in das letzte Stockwerk zu gelangen, änderte sich die Einstellung gegenüber Dachwohnungen so stark, dass sie heute beliebter sind als Wohnungen in unteren Lagen. Von einem Penthouse aus ändert sich die Perspektive, man sieht die Stadt aus einem anderen Blickwinkel. Man sieht sie von oben, ganz anders als beim Durchschreiten der Straßen. In Dachwohnungen gibt es viel Tageslicht und oft wundervolle Ausblicke. Außerdem haben viele Dachwohnungen noch Terrassen und Außenbereiche, die den Wohnkomfort und den Wert der Wohnung erhöhen. In diesem Buch stellen wir Ihnen moderne und innovative Dachwohnungen vor, die zu der Persönlichkeit ihrer Bewohner passen und bei deren Planung man die besonderen Vorteile dieses Wohnungstyps optimal zu nutzen wusste.

To live in a penthouse is to enjoy an exceptional place. The advent of the elevator, invented in the mid 19th century, brought with it a change in priorities when choosing where to live. Without the need for any physical effort to reach the top floor, penthouses saw a change in status and became highly desirable property. From a penthouse the point of view over a city changes. It can now be observed from a great height and be felt and experienced differently from when we are walking in its streets. These constructions are often bathed in light and boast excellent views. Also, on many occasions, penthouses offer terraces or other outdoor spaces, which add value to the home. This selection presents modern and innovative penthouses, which harmonize with the personality of the inhabitants and which have been designed to take full advantage of their special characteristics.

Bureau d'Architecture Olivier Dwek | Brussels, Belgium
Penthouse Churchill Abelew
Brussels, Belgium | 2005

Carl Eggermont
Apartment 70
Gent, Belgium | 2004

Core Manitto | Savona, Italy
Casa Mandorla
Savona, Italy | 2003

David Connor Design | London, UK
New Penthouse
London, UK | 2005

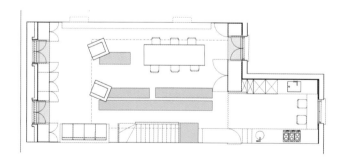

Etienne Blave | Brussels, Belgium
Loft Penthouse
Brussels, Belgium | 2003

Form Design Architecture | London, UK
Elliptical Penthouse
London, UK | 2005

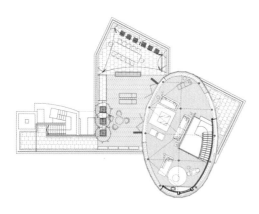

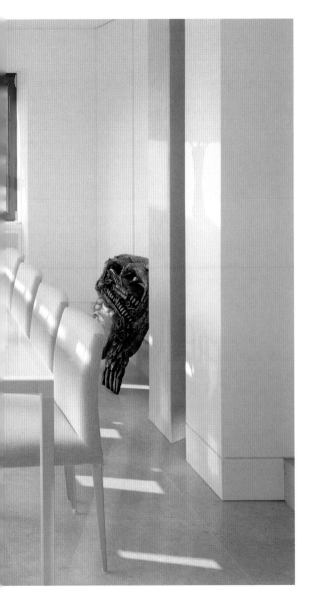

Greg Wright Architects | Cape Town, South Africa

Penthouse Pet
Cape Town, South Africa | 2003

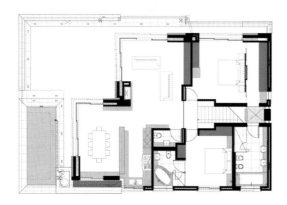

Hofman-Dujardin Architecten | Amsterdam, The Netherlands
Penthouse in Amsterdam
Amsterdam, The Netherlands | 2005

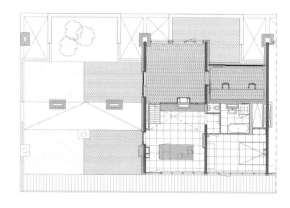

Julie Brion & Tanguy Leclercq | Brussels, Belgium
Bentley Penthouse
Brussels, Belgium | 2004

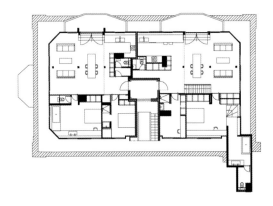

Littow Architectes | Boulogne, France
Loft Rue de Savoi
Paris, France | 2000

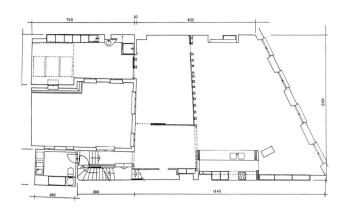

Malek-Herbst Architekten | Graz, Austria
Private Penthouse
Graz, Austria | 2006

Maroto-Ibáñez Arquitectos | Madrid, Spain
Penthouse in Madrid
Madrid, Spain | 2004

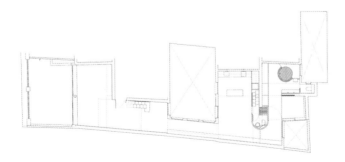

Messana-O'Rorke Architects | New York, USA
Tank House
New York, USA | 2005

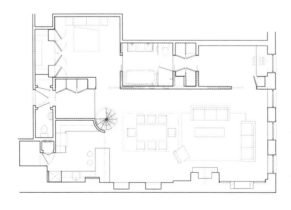

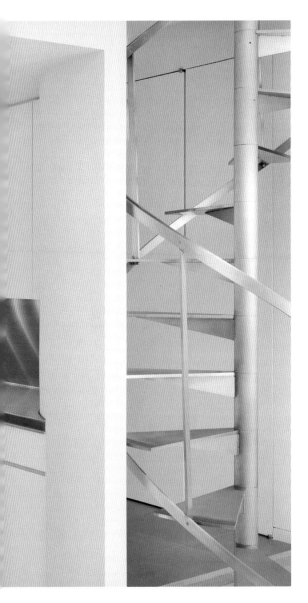

Owners
Loft Roberto
Gent, Belgium | 2004

Pagani-Dimauro Architetti | Ponte Enza, Reggio Emilia, Italy
Penthouse Matteo Combi
Parma, Italy | 2005

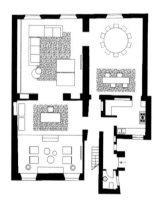

Paul Cha | New York, USA
Chelsea Duplex Penthouse
New York, USA | 2004

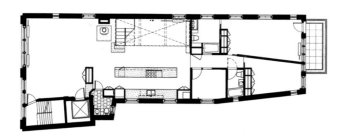

Paul Cha | New York, USA
Chelsea Loft Penthouse
New York, USA | 2004

Rogers-Marvel Architects | New York, USA
515 Canal Street Penthouse
New York, USA | 2003

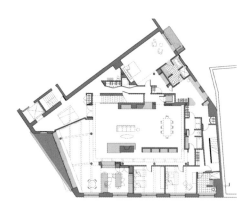

Romana Fabbris | Miami, USA
Penthouse in Miami
Miami, USA | 2001

Smith-Miller & Hawkinson Architects | New York, USA
Flynn Penthouse
New York, USA | 2004

Studio Gaia | New York, USA
Penthouse in Columbus Circle
New York, USA | 2005

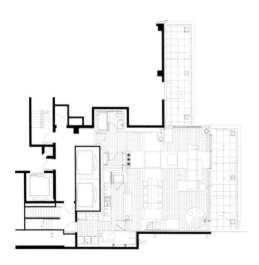

Studio MM/Mauro Manfrin | Milan, Italy
Apartment in Milan
Milan, Italy | 2005

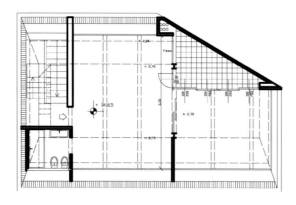

Toby Orford (owner) | Cape Town, South Africa
Hipping News
Cape Town, South Africa | 2004

Bureau d'Architecture Olivier Dwek
20 Av. du Bourg. J. Herinckx
1180 Brussels, Belgium
P +32 2 344 2804
F +32 2 344 2800
dwek.architectes@gmail.com
Penthouse Churchill Abelew
Photos: © Laurent Brandajs

Carl Eggermont
Apartment 70
Photos: © L. Wauman / Inside / Cover

Core Manitto
Via dei Vacciuoli 22 R
17100 Savona, Italy
P/F +39 0198 489460
info@coremanitto.com
www.coremanitto.com
Casa Mandorla
Photos: © Matteo Piazza

David Connor Design
10 Ivebury Court
325 Latimer Road
London W10 6RA, UK
P +44 208 964 5357
F +44 208 964 5679
info@davidconnordesign.co.uk
www.davidconnordesign.co.uk
New Penthouse
Photos: © David Connor, Kate Darby

Etienne Blave
89 b 22, rue de Linthout
1030 Brussels, Belgium
P +32 2 732 3990
F +32 2 732 0363
archeblave@skynet.be
Loft Penthouse
Photos: © Laurent Brandajs

Form Design Architecture
1 Bermondsey Exchange
179-181 Bermondsey Street
London SE1 3UW, UK
P +44 207 407 3336
Elliptical Penthouse
Photos: © Matthew Weinreb

Greg Wright Architects
8 Dixon Street, cnr Jarvis, De Waterkant
8001 Cape Town, South Africa
P +27 21 421 0417
F +27 21 421 0430
studio@gwarchitects.co.za
www.gwarchitects.co.za
Penthouse Pet
Photos: © J. de Villiers / H&L / Inside / Cover

Hofman-Dujardin Architecten
Haarlemmer Houttuinen 23
1013 GL Amsterdam, The Netherlands
P +31 2 0528 6420 / +31 6 1706 4104
F +31 2 0528 6969
office@hofmandujardin.nl
www.hofmandujardin.nl
Penthouse in Amsterdam
Photos: © Matthijs van Roon

Julie Brion & Tanguy Leclercq
204 Chaussée d'Ixelles
1050 Brussels, Belgium
M +32 47 732 0316 (J. Brion)/+32 47 969 0405 (T. Leclercq)
F +32 2 640 0018
brion.leclercq@scarlet.be
Bentley Penthouse
Photos: © Laurent Brandajs

Littow Architectes
26 bis Rue des Peupliers
92100 Boulogne, France
P +33 1 46 09 00 34
M +33 6 09 69 67 03
pekkalittow@littowarchitectes.com
www.littowarchitectes.com
Loft Rue de Savoi
Photos: © Pekka Littow

Malek-Herbst Architekten
Körösistrasse 17
8010 Graz, Austria
P +43 316 681 440 0
F +43 316 681 440 33
office@malekherbst.com
www.malekherbst.com
Private Penthouse
Photos: © Gerald Liebminger

Maroto-Ibáñez Arquitectos
Barquillo 44, 2.° der.
28004 Madrid, Spain
P +34 91 319 4523
estudio@meiarquitectos.com
www.meiarquitectos.com
Penthouse in Madrid
Photos: © Àngel Baltanàs

Messana-O'Rorke Architects
118 West 22nd Street, 9th floor
New York, NY 10011, USA
P +1 212 807 1960
F +1 212 807 1966
www.messanaororke.com
Tank House
Photos: © Elizabeth Felicella

Owners
Loft Roberto
Photos: © B. Claessens/Inside/Cover

Pagani-Dimauro Architetti
Via Emilia 14
42043 Ponte Enza, Reggio Emilia, Italy
P +39 0522 902145
F +39 0522 671826
studio@paganidimauro.com
www.paganidimauro.com
Penthouse Matteo Combi
Photos: © Matteo Piazza

Paul Cha

611 Broadway, Suite 540
New York, NY 10012, USA
P + 1 212 477 6957
F + 1 212 353 3286
mail@paulchaarchitect.com
www.paulchaarchitect.com
Chelsea Duplex Penthouse
Chelsea Loft Penthouse
Photos: © Dao Lou Zha

Rogers-Marvel Architects

145 Hudson Street, 3rd floor
New York, NY 10013, USA
P + 1 212 941 6718
F + 1 212 941 7573
www.rogersmarvel.com
515 Canal Street Penthouse
Photos: © Paul Warchol Photography

Romana Fabbris

1581 Brickell Av., Apt. T 207
Miami, FL 33129, USA
M + 1 5773 6830
rfabbris@aol.com
Penthouse in Miami
Photos: © Reto Guntli/Zapaimages

Smith-Miller & Hawkinson Architects

305 Canal Street
New York, NY 10013, USA
P + 1 212 966 3875
F + 1 212 966 3877
contact@smharch.com
www.smharch.com
Flynn Penthouse
Photos: © Matteo Piazza

Studio Gaia

401 Washington Street, 4th floor
New York, NY 10013, USA
P + 1 212 680 3500
F + 1 212 680 3535
contact@studiogaia.com
www.studiogaia.com
Penthouse in Columbus Circle
Photos: © Moon Lee/Studio Gaia

Studio MM/Mauro Manfrin

Via Viminale 6
20131 Milan, Italy
P +39 0245 488245
m.m@fastwebnet.it
Apartment in Milan
Photos: © Andrea Martiradonna

Toby Orford (owner)

Cape Town, South Africa
Hipping News
Photos: © K. Bernstein/H&L/Inside/Cover

© 2007 daab
cologne london new york

published and distributed worldwide by
daab gmbh
friesenstr. 50
d - 50670 köln

p + 49 - 221 - 913 927 0
f + 49 - 221 - 913 927 20

mail@daab-online.com
www.daab-online.com

publisher ralf daab
rdaab@daab-online.com

creative director feyyaz
mail@feyyaz.com

editorial project by loft publications
© 2007 loft publications

editor cristina paredes
layout ignasi gracia blanco
english translation jay noden
german translation susanne engler
french translation michel ficerai
italian translation maurizio siliato

printed in spain

isbn 978-3-937718-75-0